D1522546

By Joan Larkin:

HOUSEWORK, Out & Out Books, 1975

A Long Sound

A LONG SOUND

A BOOK OF POEMS

by JOAN LARKIN

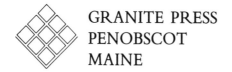

GRANITE PRESS
PENOBSCOT
MAINE

First Printing: 3000 copies, April 1986.
Cover and Book Design: Bea Gates
Cover Drawing: "Very Small Waterfall", pastel and gouache, 10" x 12", by
Sarah Jackson, courtesy of Emily Harvey Gallery, N.Y.C.
Photograph: Naomi Bushman
Set in Bem by Mary Facciolo
Paste-up: Pat McLellan
Printed on acid-free paper & smyth-sewn by
Maple-Vail Book Manufacturing Group, York, Pa.

ISBN 0-9614886-1-1
Library of Congress #:86-080225

Published by GRANITE PRESS
BOX 7, PENOBSCOT, MAINE 04476

FIRST EDITION

ACKNOWLEDGEMENTS

Poems in this collection were first published, some in different versions, in the following periodicals: *Bay Windows, Calyx, Conditions, Hanging Loose, Junction, Sailing the Road Clear, Sing Heavenly Muse!, Sinister Wisdom,* and *Sojourner.* Grateful acknowledgement is made to the editors.

"Hard Differences" was first published as a broadside in a letterpress limited edition by Bowne & Co. for the American Populist Poetry Series.

"Blood" and "Native Tongue" were included in *Lesbian Poetry: An Anthology,* ed. Elly Bulkin and Joan Larkin, Persephone Press, 1981; this anthology is distributed by Gay Press of New York.

"Sleeping on the Left Side" and "Cow's Skull with Calico Roses" were included in *Woman Poet, Volume Two: The East,* Women-in-Literature, Inc., 1981.

"The Choice," "Blood," and "Sleeping on the Left Side" were included in the LP recording *A Sign/I Was Not Alone,* Out & Out Books, 1977.

Grateful acknowledgement is made to the poet Rota Silverstrini for permission to use the line "I slept wherever night found me," which translates a line from her unpublished poem *"La Noche Prisionera,"* 1960.

The author thanks the Creative Artists Public Service Program for support at the start of the writing of this book; Naomi Bushman and Fletcher Copp for the generous use of their home in Claryville, New York, and Cummington Community of the Arts, where some of these poems were written.

Special thanks to those whose insights and encouragement made a difference during the completion of this book, especially Barbara Green, Bea Gates, Carl Morse, Edith Chevat, Honor Moore, Jane Cooper, Kate Larkin, Larry Block, Mark Ameen, Naomi Bushman, Sybil Kollar, and members of the anonymous fellowship.

for Kate Larkin

CONTENTS

  Something happened I couldn't have told you then
  You're nothing, if you've lost your precious treasure
  One after the other, the suave fuck
  Whichever, I was in his hands
  Had either of us come? I was in a blackout
  He said, Do you do this sort of thing often?
  I drank anything and slept with everyone

BROKEN GIRL

seconal and wine   I lived on the street
I slept wherever night found me
abandoned buildings   boxes   always
it wants more from you
it wants you
to drink
it doesn't mind if you die
I didn't mind

there came a night I had nothing
I went on a roof to kill myself
I prayed first   You
make the decision   let me die
or live
a long sound
Wa...   the sound of life
entered my body like a breath

held me   it was warm
a bell hung in my heart
a bell of feeling
glowed in me
then the silence   peace
it was then I got sober
after a vision you have to do it
so the next one can come to you

I want you to know this
sometimes I think I won't make it
yesterday voices were singing
kill yourself   this
goes on for years after the drugs
right now I'm alive   grateful
if you find it hard to believe
look at me

I Blood

NATIVE TONGUE

My first language was wet
and merging.
My syllables were not distinct
from hers; our liquid interface
floated my slow vowels
in the infradark
of her hold,

my serious fish   face
my belly with its tendril
registering her depth
charges.

My first language was light
split by white slats
into molten series
buzzing with dust—
light on my dry, new body.

Vaseline,
clean worm on mama's finger
on my vulva
while I lay, white diaper, white
chenille spread, legs across the edge
of the big bed.

My first language was food:
thin, warm thread of milk
dull oatmeal in a pewter bowl,
gingerbread—round boys with raisin eyes,
grandma smiling, standing at the iron stove
with its porcelain cocks and nipples.

The dog's breathing and the dog's dry tongue—
she was and was not a person.
Dirty they said, but told
how she was Celia's
good girl.
Her high bark
sliced thin portions of the cold.
She was my size.

I was smaller than the steep words
around me: tommy gun, stolen,
hitler. Mother is a nurse's
aide, father is an air raid warden
in the dark cellar. His helmet
is white and important.

We are jews. There are bombs,
oil, an icebox, a victory
garden. You can count by twos
in your hand with fat green seeds.

BLOOD

You mix flesh, your first time with his paintbox:
raw sienna, white, a squeeze of red.
His knife spreads grease rainbows on the palette.
What will you do, now that your father's dead—

you of my poems, whose eyes swallow me
whole, like the dark that drank Persephone—
you spread the paint with delicate bloody strokes
on a large redlipped woman you say is me.

You ripened in my blood like a red fruit
until you split the air with your separate breath.
Then I could not protect you from the fathers;
nor can I bear for you now this father's death.

We paint each other large: daughter, mother,
images delivered of each other's dark.
I've drunk the light of your hair. You've swallowed hell
and can survive the ways it wants you back.

THE CHOICE

When they choose abortion for you
and the plane shakes your heart like a ballot
and the dream of the baby blackens like plants
and your father advises like the clearest ice
and your mother turns you over like a sheet
and the doctor smiles like iron
and your womb delivers a bowl of blood
to the mouth of the toilet announcing *Nothing*
and the salt draws like a poultice on the red
howl inside you, and the red clot
drops like a dish on a dumbwaiter, then
it's a dead story.

TUESDAY

My swollen will holds on like this idiot litter.
Dozing flies, the runt, the dust, nothing
can lift itself. The sky thickens like cheese.
I suffer with the cows. They weigh the air with their tails,
stand at the fence, i.d.'s wired through their ears—
what got them up is gone. In the damp bales,
nothing is breathing. Sub-creatures, specks of pepper,
crawl on the clover. I keep forgetting the date.
Night drops and the moon: sac full of blood.
I whine and drone. *To be smashed flat—to stain.*
Before morning, a bobcat claws at the quiet.
Barometers drop. A barn door cries, sways open.
An upper light flicks on. A tapedeck. News.
The throaty plumbing mourns, the cistern floods.

OPEN QUESTION

In your curved house
(take care of, take care),
as the tender column of your neck
turned, as you slept
(take care)—
still unsolved,

was your soul scraped free
of your body *(take care)*
like the last jot
of dependent flesh
the curette freed
from my clinging womb?

FAWN BEFORE BOW SEASON

The day I went to work,
I stopped nursing you, I pushed
the thick rubber nipple between your lips.
Something in your eyes' dark lakes
disappeared—did I really see this?
Daily you were drenching ten pounds
of diapers, bedclothes. You weighed
nothing. Puffball.
I held you in the crook of one arm.
Your small breath warmed me.
Work at the computer billing company
began at nine. The sitter
could give you bottles. When I was done
paying her, there was money
for one week's food—
I knew this was true,
even when Jim said, *That job
costs you more than you take home.*

Tonight,
end of August, you are eighteen.
I'm fine, you repeat on the phone.
There's a cool edge to the air,
the season turning. It's dusk.
From my open car window, I see
the fawn, head lifted, half
over the fence. For a moment,
she moors me in her dark gaze—
then floats back, soundless,
somewhere I can't see.
Nothing I know can hold her in the field.

II   Talk To Me

GENEALOGY

I come from alcohol.
I was set down in it like a spark in gas.
I lay down dumb with it, I let it erase what it liked.
I played house with it, let it dress me, undress me.
I exulted, I excused.
I married it. And where it went, I went.
I gave birth to it.
I nursed, I plotted murder with it.
I laid its table, paid its promises.
I lived with it wherever it liked to live:
in the kitchen, under the bed, at the coin laundry,
out by the swings, in the back seat of the car,
at the trashed Thanksgiving table.
I sat with it in the blear of tv.
I sat where it glittered, carmine,
where it burned in a blunt glass,
where it stood in a glittering lineup on the bar.
I saw it in the dull mirror, making up my face,
in the week-end silence,
in the smashed dish, in the slammed car door,
in the dead husband, the love.
Alcohol in the torn journal.
Alcohol in the void mirror.
My generations are of alcohol
and all that I could ever hope to bear.

CLIFTON

I loved booze,
and booze and pills I loved more.
I still love them.
I still want them.
My wine, my Dexamil,
my after-dinner tall
tumbler of scotch,
my morning black espresso,
my Valium at work,
and more Valium.
It worked.
The Dexamil let me drink,
the drink kept me from feeling,
the Valium kept my hand from shaking.
The Dexamil let me drink
in the face of my psychiatrist saying,
I think you drink too much—
I think I won't see you if you drink.
In the face of fines,
in the face of swinging at a cop,
in the face of connecting with a two-by-four,
in the face of cops looking down at me in the middle of
                                        Amsterdam Avenue
in a Brooks Brothers suit, a briefcase,
in the *middle* of Amsterdam Avenue—
Where do you live, sir? We think you should go home.

I drank at Hanratty's for four reasons:
it's near where I live,
they cashed my checks,
they closed at one,

and they took me home.
At home, I would have another
scotch and a pill,
at 5:30 get up,
drink coffee, take a pill—
I had—I have—
a responsible job.
I was always first at my desk
and last to leave.
I never wanted to work.
I wanted someone else to take care of it all.

I don't know why I'm alive today.
I don't believe in God, I'm a strict Freudian.
When I stopped, I thought,
This is unspeakable deprivation.
I whined and cried.
I sat in the back eleven months
pitying myself. Home
from a dinner with board members,
with two glasses of wine, the first in a year—
I opened the half bottle of scotch
a guest had left. It was months under the sink.
Often I'd thought of it. Always,
I knew it was there.
I poured scotch into a tumbler,
and I couldn't drink it.
I couldn't. I thought, *I can't go through all that again.*

That was ten years ago.
My hair is gray. A doorman
with whom I left a package yesterday
described me to my friend as "distinguished."
Lots of things are the same.
Some things are changed, changing.

I love booze in my dreams.
I drink booze and take pills in my dreams.
I don't ask *Why*
do I love alcohol? Instead,
I have habits strict as the former ones,
meetings, books, service.
The dreams full of booze keep telling me what I am.

Late in my life,
in the numb elegance of this city,
I made a decision—
or the decision
shining in the soft, brutal darkness
took hold of me—
to live.
Often I am peaceful.
I never imagined that.

GOOD-BYE

You are saying good-bye to your last
drink. There is no lover
like her: bourbon, big gem
in your palm and steep
fiery blade in your throat,
deadeye down. None like her
but her sister, first
gin, like your first
seaswim, first woman
whose brine took to your tongue,
who could change the seasons of your cells
like nothing else.
Unless it was wine, finally
your only companion, winking
across the table, hinting
in her rubies, her first-class labels,
of her peasant blood
and the coarse way she would open you.

Good-bye, beauties. You don't want to say it.
You try to remember
the night you fell out of the car
and crawled to the curb, the night
two of you stood
screaming over your daughter's crib.
You remember deaths
by gin, by easy capsules—
the friend who fell in silence
and the friend who quoted *Antony* in his suicide note.
All this helps for a moment, till your heart
blooms and stiffens with desire.

IN WESTERN MASSACHUSETTS, SIXTEEN MONTHS SOBER

The first year I was out here, because there were no flowers I began picking up bones.

—Georgia O'Keeffe

To find words for this.

There's a tree. And its shadow.
And a wind washing the shadow
uphill through the weeds.

Once you said to me,
There's a word for everything.
Words
I don't trust now.

I'm walking uphill—
no fiction.

Phrasebook of a country I'm visiting.
I remember the names from before.
Goldenrod, cricket. The cedar waxwing.
Driving downhill, a couple. Backseat, the kids.
The field blows toward me hard.

The late light chooses
white stones in the wall,
a white moth, and the white leaf
turning.

To simplify—
I tore so many papers.

Briefly
it was winter. Then
in Brooklyn, at the bottom of my house,
someone in the mirror
wearing my plaid robe,
still asking to be carried.

Walking home, the low sun
on my bare arms.
Outside the blind piano tuner's house
air stirs the flag,
a pony trots,
a boy watches his sister.

Francis, a year ago you asked,
Do you have the willingness to be happy?
I can't always say.
Today
I'm climbing this hill,
I'm picking up
this pen.

CO-ALCOHOLIC

I saw you in the street, head lowered, stumbling;
I waited two years to call.
This is the last time, I told myself.
Unless he's dead, I'll tell him about the fellowship.
This time, no ice against glass against my ear—
"I'm sober," you said.

You were trembling, pallid,
your fat a cradle around you,
the old tattoo like a bruise purpling your arm.
You kept trying to kiss me.
"I need someone I don't have to impress," you said.
Should. Shouldn't. I judged myself without pity.

You remembered 1969, an acid trip,
the *I Ching* hexagrams we'd formed, fucking.
Above, the clinging, fire; below, wind and wood.
Lake over fire: molting, an animal's pelt.
Last night, the rose and bruise-purple of my cunt
were the colors in my mind's eye

of slick internal shapes twisting and coupling,
Blake's underworld river, looped like a gut.
Above, the abysmal, water,
below, the receptive, earth—
hair glistening like oil
on your thin chest my breasts wilted on.
Last night the fear in my eyes stared at the fear in your eyes.

I came down from Lowell to see Brad.
I was working late shifts alone,
no one to speak to, machines
slick and dangerous. Staying
at my parents' again, like velvet handcuffs.
I borrowed the silver Skylark.
I remember me the

blonde, twenties, eyes
clouded over, face
like dough left standing, gray.
Did I think anything?

I parked. I got there
just as the weekend drinking
was getting off the ground.
I think they were glad to see me.

I remember bits. Vodka,
lots of it. Some musical
I passed out in. Brad's dad
patting my shoulder in a downtown
bar, buying us
boilermakers. Joan and Brad
in that lurid light, leaving us,
leaving me Joan's keys—
which I lost. Me trying to scale
their building at four a.m.,
coming to on the subway tracks,
head resting on the wood
guard for the third rail,

me on the train, getting a whiff
of my pissed pants, my bloodied hair,
no jacket, no car keys, no license, no memory
of where the car was.

We drank
what was left of Sunday.
Brad's father had my jacket, keys,
i.d.—everything was great!
Except that I'd missed work
and was out of money
and my body had several bruises,
I wasn't sure where from.

The weekend was over.
One minute
I was in the left lane on the Mass Pike,
next thing I was drifting toward the guard rail.

It wasn't going to be easy
getting home.

A QUALIFICATION: PAT H.

I talked to the bathtub.
It was made of atoms;
atoms were alive, I reasoned,
so the tub was alive—
it was my friend.
Sometimes I fell into it.
Oh but I didn't bathe—
I stank in those days.
I talked to it for hours,
also to the Barbra Streisand poster on the door.
I'd sit facing it—
my six-pack next to me in the sink—
drinking, pissing, for hours.
At least then I wasn't pissing on *her*
or in those goddamn shorts.
It's a miracle I'm here to tell you this:
all those years I tried to be dead.

One doctor said I was premenstrual,
one diagnosed grand mal epilepsy
and let me go. *I'm sick!*
I thought, and got some vodka down.
One day I sat looking at the glass in my hand
and I knew. It was that sudden.
Something wanted to live;
it wasn't me.
How the message got through
my fog   my denial
I can't tell you.
There has to be a higher power.
Still, no instant change.
I fought recovery.

I had one slip five years ago
and tried to kill myself.
It was when my mother died—
I won't go into it.
It's different now.

It hurts to say all this.
I need you. Talk to me.
How does my life remind you of your own?

The sky cracks along
a branch of sycamore: its fault.
The sidewalk, split in jigsaw-
puzzle pieces by the roots,
lifts, oblique to itself.
The foreground—leaves and bark—
collapses like a sinkhole
while the sky's crazed blue
bulges like heavy crockery.
Everything seems to have two
sides. I could be wrong.

III   I Couldn't Have Told You

"Then I floated solitary in no-world."

—Elizabeth Malloy

It was a party; I had on my party dress.
There was something wrong in Grandpa's friend's throat.
I kept him waiting outside the bathroom
while I read *Mother West Wind "When" Stories.*
When Mama yelled at me to *Make it fast,*
I wiped. I flushed. I came out on the landing
holding the blue book behind my back.
His lighted cigar was the red eye of an animal.
He reached a hand up—big, spotted like an animal—
under the short skirt of my party dress.
I felt pleasure, and I felt afraid of the hand.
Nice girl, he was smiling,
and the red eye shook and smelled like a cigar.
This was at the top of some stairs—
what house was it?
Were there stairs on Westminster Avenue?
How little was I? I remember. Little.
I said, *Mama, the man touched me.*
No, she said. She was worried
about the party; she was serving
a tray of green things and pink things.
She explained the facts to me quickly.
No, she said.
The man is a nice old man.

RAPE

After twenty years I want to call it that, but was it?
I mean
it wasn't all his fault, I mean
wasn't I out there on 8th Street,
wandering around looking for someone to fill the gap where my center
                                                                  would have been?
Didn't I circle the same block over & over until he saw me?
Wasn't I crying when he came along & said *Don't do that, cops
                              see me with a white girl crying*—
I'm sorry. Didn't I say *I'm sorry,* & didn't I smile?
Didn't I walk with him, dumb, to the Hotel Earle,
didn't I drink with him in his room,
didn't I undress myself in the stare of a yellow bulb?
Didn't I drink—what was it I drank?
Didn't I drink enough to be numb for a long time?
Didn't I drink myself into a blackout?

Was it rape, if when I lay there letting him fuck me I started
                                                              to feel
sore & exhausted & said *Stop,*
first softly, then screaming
Stop, over & over?
And if he was too drunk to hear me,
or if he heard me but thought, *Girls never mean it when they say stop,*
was that rape? Was it rape if he meant well
or was too drunk to hear me, was it rape
if he kept repeating *Girl, you can fuck*
& not really meaning any harm?

I think I remember that the room was green & black,

44

the small bulb dangling from a cord,
the bed filthy.
I don't exactly remember.
I know I had no pleasure, but lay there; I don't think he forced me.
It was just that he wouldn't stop when I asked him to.
He didn't take my money.
It may have been his booze I drank.
It may have been sort of a date.
He wrote his number on half a matchbook & said
Call Joe if you need him—I guess he was Joe.

Did I walk home?
Did I have any money?
Was it me who bought the booze?
Maybe I took a cab.
Was it 2:00 a.m., or safe daylight
when I climbed the five flights,
spent, feeling the tear tracks & pounded cervix,
the booze still coating me, my nerves not yet awake, stripped &
                                                    screaming.
I climbed to my place, five flights,
somehow satisfied,
somehow made real by the pain.

Was it rape, then?

BOUND

Full moon in Libra pulls you from the bed.
You're drunk, hurt, angry, wanting to talk
but not trusting words. *I'm sick of words,* you say,
turning your back when I beg you to tell me what
it is: your love for Jill? Some jealousy? Your hate
of me tonight—of you? Your brother's call?
Your thesis advisor's telling you, after you'd cracked
the code of *Moby Dick* & given the best oral defense
in the school's history (he admits it), in the posh
office where he's studying Shirley Temple—his saying, *Learn shorthand.*
Live like a faculty wife. Be
a woman. You told me this yesterday, quiet-voiced.
This is one ripple. In your lake of moonlit nightmare
you lie dumb, bound in barbed wire. You won't move.

BLACKOUT SONNETS

Something happened I couldn't have told you then.
He was dark, with a beak like Uncle Ben's,
another salesman in a suit. Barry, my music teacher's son—
a senior, hot when I was twelve, Book One
propped on the instrument.
Now I was eighteen. My mother was intent
about my hem and hair. On her knees,
mouth full of pins, she spit out sharp advice:
Don't overdo the makeup. Face
facts: you've got my hips. She was amazed
a plausible, tall Jew would date
her daughter. I was damaged goods. Too late
to do me any good, she'd said last year,
You're nothing, if you've lost your precious treasure.

You're nothing, if you've lost your precious treasure.
So I guess I gave him nothing, on the sofa
in his parents' finished basement (big tv,
plush carpet, bar) listening, New Year's eve,
to his favorite Gershwin—which we had to hear
twice. Zero degrees, I felt numb about the year
1957. His folks, a blur
of blue cigar smoke and a full-length fur,
were climbing into the Caddy as we drove in:
Goodnight—I was unprepared. She still looked grim
as when I hadn't practised, which was most
of the time. Barry, the conscientious host,
opened two bottles of sparkling Cold Duck
one after the other—the suave fuck.

One after the other, the suave fuck
followed the fake champagne. I wasn't struck
by the way I took his cues; only his taste
appalled me. Eighteen, I was a wine-snob, based
on one date with a transfer student from Paris.
Cold Duck fluorescent in my blood, black dress
hiked to my hips, my pale pink synthetic
panties spilled on the rug, his tireless prick
battering my numbed entrance—I couldn't say
whether or not I wanted it that way.
For all I know, we would have gone someplace—
dancing, a movie—if, in my half-a-voice,
I'd said, *No more thanks.* Or *What are your plans?*
Whichever, I was in his hands.

Whichever, I was in his hands—
what shit. I wanted him inside my pants.
I knew my lines and hurried through them. Once
drunk, I could direct him, no coy hints,
to close the coffin and then nail me in—
that was the point. Fucking put a lid on pain
like nothing since the rubber cone of ether
on my nose and mouth that night last year.
Saline injection, hot curette in my womb,
blood in the toilet, mother screaming in my room—
the whole damned family was in on it.
Brother, cousin—all of them suffered the secret.
Now Barry flickered and passed out.
Had either of us come? I was in a blackout.

Had either of us come? I was in a blackout.
It was two when I woke up in the Buick on Route
Nine. I stared at the immaculate floor,
carpeted to match dark maroon leather
upholstery. My high heels pierced the shag.
I fished inside my black patent bag
for keys and hoped my mother was in bed.
Barry drove without turning his head.
My pants were soaked. I shivered, though the heat
was blasting. Queasy—*We didn't even eat—*
I clung to my cold keys and stared at signs
and Barry's profile, trying to read his mind.
And in a tone he might have meant to soften,
he said, *Do you do this sort of thing often?*

He said, *Do you do this sort of thing often?*
No—I could barely say it. My face stiffened.
It sickens me even now, remembering this:
I had been hoping for a goodnight kiss.
Skidding on new snow, the Buick turned
my corner. Barry clammed up. The cold burned
as he opened the door on my side, courteous,
distant: he had had nothing to do with this.
I grabbed his cashmere sleeve and climbed the icy
steps to the squat brick house I
hated; my folks had moved here right
after the abortion. September, a soft night,
Uncle's knife scraped out my next-of-kin.
Now I drank anything and slept with everyone.

I drank anything and slept with everyone
and kept my mouth shut about the abortion.
I hardly remember 1957—
I stopped speaking to my closest friend
when her boyfriend called me up and said, *I want
your doctor's name.* His sleeve soft, my cunt
sore, we climbed the stairs to 7-B.
Mom opened the door and stared at me
as if I were a mirror. Was my dress
zipped only part way up? Barry glanced at us,
looking supremely sane, said a smooth *Goodnight,*
and left. Her laugh a snort, *You're good and late!*
she said, and *Will he ask you out again?—*
and something happened I couldn't have told you then.

IV   Where I Set It Down

RING

It was late, it was just before work—
and I thought I had lost my mother's
ring! Running from room
to room, I thought of all
I had lost: I broke my mother's
cut-glass dish, unraveled
her patient afghan—endless
worm from one pink
string—the things I had ruined!
Sloven, I let the dog in,
left the garbage boiling
with maggots, the gas on, the plugged-in
iron heating the house.
Engines idled everywhere I turned
keys. Meters were ticking,
taps bleeding. The kettle
screeched. The house
was flooding, stuffing itself
with steam. In the cellar, oil
was inching, fattening the stone floor
into loam. As I ran from bedroom
to bathroom to bedroom, facing
the blind drawers, the grinning
drain, floorboards wincing
and crying, the tall house
was thickening like spores
in your throat once you eat
the death cup, white
Amanita. The taste exploding
in my pink mouth, *You're dead,*
my friend, I said to myself,
and, too late,
found it just where I set it down.

WATERCOLOR: FROM THE CABIN

Light dissolves the screen so I don't see it,
the door's an H framing the weeds,
green blazes over green—
a minute. This day's a banging shutter.
Open, it shows what's whitest:
plastic jug like a pale light on the stump;
stones in the graveyard;
downhill a door, a roof, barn windows;
the purple-martin house (four staring portholes);
now the turned edge of every blade, in a wind.
It's still again. A minute.
A wash of silver milk gives way to black,
breaks open a blue shape, seals itself.
White sky: dome full of liquid—nothing spilled.

A slight thing crawls
to the cabbage-heart,
swells with cabbage-leaf,
becomes cabbage,
lies on my plate, pale
glisten of green juice
in a world called worm.
Claryville
swells in me, new word
uncurling on my tongue.
Summer. The warm rain
rises to the tops of stones;
the throat of the brook fills;
its dark, slick skin
unwrinkles, wrinkles.
A hand is smoothing things—
dust of winged bodies
under a lamp,
blue-black trunk of the spruce
in its pool of shadow,
slug gleaming on my sandal.
Cavities fill with blood,
the bud of the breast,
the bud of the clitoris
plumped like pink beans
or the curled, filled
larvae feeding, feeding.
Small gold apples
are shaken like drops
as if there were no mistakes.

COW'S SKULL WITH CALICO ROSES

Nothing soft in this skull
hung up, somewhere—
so it appears in this print
though to be painted
it must have been laid on cloths.
The black split between two continents
of white linen
could be O'Keeffe's table.

Sheets—softly folded
petals of flesh—
or abstraction:
white labia
or a white cello
fretted with thick silk stems
of a calico rose
concealing the cow's jawbone.

It's hard to see things
as they are said not to be,
but harder
not to see the cross
imposed on this flat sheet,
the split in this
tradition of painted space
she chooses.

She takes West to its limit
in this picture. Bleached
needlework flowers
hint of women's hands,
hot afternoons.

Hard not to see
the farmhouse, white
blister on the land.

Christ could be in this,
or the painter's faith
in desert light.
But I see an abortion—
papers torn to bits
with words on them—
a body fretted
by an unlike nature.

A disappearance, an abyss—
in this skull shaped like a pelvis
cracked in the center,
the black vertical plummeting
into a calico spiral,
the unlikely collaboration
of things to outlast a life:
its artifacts and bones.

CONFIDENCE

One witch to another winks, you told me yesterday.
& all is winking in this place,
its women passing through it who've loved you, love you—
many.
I want to be the eye of this concentric loveliness
but *Who can compete with the Goddess?* you seem to be saying.
You claim your love's reluctant to limit Her variety.
We ate fish stew last night. You mentioned *class difference*
making me wonder which of us had more royalty
in her flaming eyes. Right now I walk circles around things:
my foot's gone to sleep. The dogs
watch me as I mutter my lines aloud.
Will poems witch-wink to you on the hill?
I think they will.

STRUCK

You got me scared right off the bat
with your saying you'd like me to buy this house
& you'd had a hot love affair with a strong woman—
a quick confession. You're as reckless as I am.
You say you love me, you're happy I'm here. You say, Come
spend the summer; I may go to Minnesota though.
On my own so fast! I think, staring at the tadpoles—
there are thousands wriggling in this little lake
with everything in it, near it, above it, stirring
fin, wing, tail. I rub the dog, you rub my leg, we talk
& groom ourselves like seals against each other.
Your thoughts shock me like last night's lightning
striking right by the house. The house rolls
& your cups in the kitchen's thunder peal as they fall.

FOWLER BEACH

We lie facing the parted dunes,
blue thunder at our backs,
the gulls aloft, aroused, loud,
a low plane ripping out a seam.
All the boys have oiled their swank bodies,
their litter—wrappers, filter butts—
tumbled with fluted stone
wings of scallops
and the clean bones of clams.

ALBA

Weeping, I twist awake, won't tell you what:
a pink fizz drink I didn't want,
wet pants, my frozen tongue, my wasted brother....
You hold me in your sleep's surface tension
until the buzzer rips you from my text.

No laughs allowed as you groan, *I forgot my toothbrush,*
swiveling into jeans that mean business.
The past is past: pitch of my cry, coming,
that keyed your nerves' flash flood at 3:00 a.m.

Later, it could snow. Now you go out, in the pink
first light of a clean borough. Through a clear pane,
All Saints cuts the white sky like cake,
that cloud's a dragon snorkeling through the spires.
Cold angels watch you—there's a gull—and bless.

WOMEN'S BARRACKS

Tray of expensive medicine on top,
mirror doubling the cleft pills,
the comb & brush set I hated twice,
fake metals back to back

& the deep sliders full of white
nighties, nylons, gift links,
lilac soap, still wrapped—I touched
each thing, pulse up as I stole

Women's Barracks from shining folds
of a slip. I hadn't touched my self
yet, but what could equal this
for grownup stuff & Daddy back of it.

A THREAD

Your sister died—

Did you let in your own grief
or did you wind yourself up tight
on the spool of your mother's pain

Are you still taking care of your mother

Tell me the story
again
so we both can hear
how it all comes out

V All Parts of the Body

A KISS

The hardness
with which you still hate
your body

is a kiss for the fathers.

BECAUSE AGAIN

You entered me. I was afraid
that Spanish song in the street
was the whole story:
mi corazón! it cried as usual
numbing my legs into uselessness. *Beautiful*
you were saying, and I couldn't breathe.
I was a clam,
closed, no throat, and hair of stone,
in the dark drapery of your breast—

mi corazón, o flesh, and stamp of prison.

SLEEPING ON THE LEFT SIDE

"I *primaled* it," she said,
the smooth word like "marbled"
embarrassing me.

She remembered
being kept
from the camps—
she was three.
On that field at the edge
of death
her mother kissed her,
her father did not
look
up. Thirty years
later, the Dutch woman
said, "Yes, it did happen
that way
when I saved you."

"But what
about the side?
Did you wake me that year
so I wouldn't sleep
on my left side?"

"That side gives bad
dreams, they say,
and you had nightmares
every night—we had to turn you
over."

Her nightmares are over,
she tells me:
they rose to her
throat—she screamed—
she "primaled" them
away.

But for me, her dreams
are just beginning—
her mother's kiss—unfinished—
her father's bent head.

A TASTE

I thought the sweetest fruit must be a plum
with its dark-veined polish

inside there were gold, green, pink

the taste: lush unripe teasweet salt-sour
suck of wholeness I don't tire of

A BURNING

Black kites
spiral above the sink,
lift in a draft,

are driven from their wits,
then dizzy, slow
& drop

like dead moths' wings,
powder
too light to collect   in the windy kitchen.

Words in the ashes,
handwriting, still visible
in the sloughed skin:

the woman who immolated herself—
in London—something about her son
I can't remember

& can't remember
what was in this journal
sacrificed years back—

one or two dreams:
the one where Mom insists on a spiral staircase,
her tone a case of murder,

& the dream of a ship's hold,
one room warm & muted for the men,
one where women move in a blaze of crystal.

This fire's an offering to the husband,
whatever he wants—
it's the opposite of wanting

not to lie. In any case,
I'm burning. It's what I do,
today this page,

suttee done in the kitchen,
tomorrow touching
some other match.

SELF-LOVE

Breast to my breast
I held my beloved
with both hands
her breath
came through my house
closed eyes re/member
river   cinnamon fern
sea cave and wet
conch unburied by my fingers
from pulling mud

I make my body   sing
I am the potter and the spinning clay
She sings: I center
I put my two hands to myself
and heal all this

TRANSLATION

No truthful way to say just
how the wood thrush swayed on the limb
repeating her short phrase,
your hair threaded my fingers,
your back against my palm, your neck—
salt fallen into honey.
The hieroglyphic
of a crisp hair in my hand.

NOTES ON SEX WITHOUT LOVE

It's possible.
Like a Xerox or a Nutrasweet,
a backup file, a Macy's
Santa or a forced laugh.
It can be purely mechanical:
forward, backspace, decrease speed, delete,
& don't fumble the opening-menu options.
Fucking—a solo spacewalk.
Any appearance of spontaneous
courage or lust to the contrary,
it's a trope. A rite of warding-off.
Tough, prophylactic as see-through
cellophane on a box of gassed tomatoes.
Noli me tangere in its newest forms:
Voice Classifieds, or a cervical cap,
no strings attached.

HARD DIFFERENCES

Your face
like a map of mountains

your body
creviced, blushing
with its dark aureoles

Aetna, Vesuvius...
Monadnock—
something volcanic and Latin
crashes against my Massachusetts rock

or the opposite

my lust
pilgrim to your stone
Roman-emperor heart
moated by oceans

The frog croaks on my pillow, *Kiss. Kiss.*
It can't listen.
I created this.
The green skin glistens.

It can't listen.
I hate what I obey.
The green skin glistens—
this is a token body.

I hate what I obey.
It's so soft.
This is a token body.
Why hasn't it left?

It's so soft
I touch it. It croaks.
Why hasn't it left?
I kiss it, it pops—*Don't look.*

I touch it, it croaks.
In public it's human.
I kiss it, it pops. Don't look
now. It says it's a prince.

In public it's human;
I created this.
Now it says it's a prince,
the frog croaks on my pillow, *Kiss. Kiss.*

THE POWER OF NAMING

Kathleen Greenwell, Ph.D., say the cards from your brother.
Corky, says the women-writers'-conference list—
like a camp nickname, I think. A lake,
a wooded environment, the psychic reader reminds me.
The power of naming! you say. *It stuns me, over & over.*
You point out the strawberry magnet on the refrigerator
& say, *It starts there, with that wink at a thing,*
that eyepop: surprise. Next step's to compare two things.
I say, "Your tongue" is like "thinking of the lake"— a local instance—
Cow dogwood, you say. *Its name's a nexus. Two eyelevels.*
Now, you finish, *you say the name over & over. Lesbian planet,*
you invent. Yesterday you said, *Women name the weeds.*
Mouse Ear Chickweed. Sourgrass. Dead Man's Hand.
I've got to get a name & settle down.

.

HOW THE HEALING TAKES PLACE

How the face changes, the cloud
you'd skim from a pot of lentils
comes clear, how the gaze
comes clear as honey when you heat it,
how the eyes surrender their fear,
dark lake of beach plums
boiled for jam. How flesh

yields new flesh, lips
softening like soaked beans.
How the puffed skin settles,
dough becomes bread,
its brown, delicate grain.
How the dead hair—that mouse,
matted and stiff in the trap—
grows sleek again. How the thoughts,

like black ants going
and coming from the mouse's corpse,
go slower. How the torn mind
puts forth tendrils.
How the gray house of the lungs,
frayed and weather-beaten,
fills with moist breath.
How the breath brings healing

to all parts of the body.
To the salt rivers of blood,
to the many-tiered skeleton,
to the breast, beaded and creased,
humming like wings in the jewel-weed,
to the softening belly,
to the thick, unfurling petals of the sex.

How everything speaks—
hands unclenching—
heart.
How the belly will lift its flat
stone, the tears roll
stones from entrances.

NOTES

"In Western Massachusetts, Sixteen Months Sober": The epigraph is from the soundtrack of Perry Miller's film celebrating the life and work of Georgia O'Keeffe.

Part III, *"I COULDN'T HAVE TOLD YOU"*: The epigraph, "Then I floated solitary in no-world," is taken from Elizabeth Malloy, "Myth for a Winter's Eve," in *Lesbian Nuns: Breaking Silence,* ed. Rosemary Curb & Nancy Manahan (The Naiad Press, 1985).

"A Burning": The phrase *"suttee* done in the kitchen" was suggested by the practice of bride-burning in India today, the burning to death of a recently married young woman by the groom's family in order to get a second dowry when there is not enough income from the marriage. Often the victim is taken by surprise in the kitchen. These kitchen murders are discussed by Veena Talwar Oldenburg in "Women Against Women or Culture Against Women?: Notes on the Current Pathology of the Dowry System in Urban North India," a paper presented at the 1984 New York State Asian Conference, SUNY Cortland, October 13, 1984.

"Notes on Sex Without Love": The phrase *"Noli me tangere"* (Touch me not) is echoed from a sonnet by Sir Thomas Wyatt which begins "Whoso list to hunt: I know where is an hind" (ca. 1527). In Wyatt's sonnet, a deer symbolizing an elusive lover wears these words (quoted by Wyatt from John 20:17) on a diamond collar.

Joan Larkin was born in Boston, Massachusetts, in 1939, and attended Swarthmore College and the University of Arizona. She has lived in Brooklyn and taught writing at Brooklyn College since 1969. She has taught poetry workshops in Maine, Massachusetts, Florida, and at Sarah Lawrence College. She helped to found Out & Out Books, a women's independent publishing company active from 1975 to 1981, and co-edited the anthologies *Amazon Poetry* and *Lesbian Poetry* with Elly Bulkin. Her first book of poetry is called *Housework*. She has a daughter, Kate.

Granite Press entered trade publishing in the fall of 1985 to expand distribution and widen exposure of essential writing by feminists and lesbians. Previously, the press operated as a letterpress printshop, designing jobs and publishing poetry chapbooks and broadsides by women. We will continue to publish poetry and short stories and remain committed to clear and exciting book design. We welcome your support.